786 Sufi Wisdom
Divine Mind Science- Sufi Meditation
- by Qiyamah Abdallah Salihu – sufi

–

ༀ་མ་ཎི་པདྨེ་ཧཱུྃ

Table of contents

1. The student

2. Who/HU am "I"

3. Why am I here?

4. The Path

5. Light upon Light

6. My mother used to say

7. The eagle and the chicken

8. Half empty or Half full

9. Divine Mind

10 Divine Mind Science

11 Happiness IS

786 Sufi Wisdom Copyright @ 2012

786...The Student

When the student is ready

the teacher will appear

Have no fear

God is here!

You ask where?

Existing in you as you

clouds of the mind

GET in the way

Somehow we all forget that

We are beings of light

Having a human Experience

True self exist beyond time and physical

form

learn to laugh when others cry

life is like a divine paradox

God is looking for God and

you are in the way

be still and know.

786

Who am I?

Everyone knows that the ocean contains the drop. Few know that the drop contains the ocean. That which comes from perfection is perfect. A perfect artist paints a perfect picture. You or I may see flaws in the painting, but the perfect artist sees it as perfect. The illustrious Buddah has said " 99% of our problems only exist in the mind." When you ask yourself " Who am I," the mind paints a false picture of who you are based on your life's past experience and false ideas and beliefs about the self. If your definition of self and answer to the question "Who am I" have anything to do with race, gender, age, religion, or culture, then your answer is related to the false self and not the true self.

We all have two selves: the false self and the true self. Most people live their entire life from the personality of the false self and never learn to identify with the true self. The false self is the self that was created by the society you live in and the experiences of your life. In most cases the true self becomes like a star actor in a play who's part was stolen by a younger up and coming actor.

The true self is beyond birth and death, immortal, and not effected by the storms and trials of life.

The true self is not related to the 5 senses. The true self is not the body, mind, emotions, or desires. The true self is not related to race, gender, or religion. The true self is a Light from God that lives in the heart of all beings. The true Self is the silent witness of the movie that we call life.

People always ask "How do we know that this true Self exists?" The true

Self never sleeps, and exists above and beyond the mind. When you are sound asleep and the body and mind have shut down, the true self is there as the witness of the dream state. When you have a dream and awaken form deep sleep, who is it that tells the dream to the mind? It is the true Self!

Who am I? I am the true Self, an eternal being of light (soul), existing beyond birth and death, living in the heart, having a human experience.

786

Why am I here?

The nature of the true Self is truth (SAT), consciousness (CHI), and bliss (ANANDA). I once asked a yogi mystic how could I find happiness. He looked at me, smiled and replied "Happiness is not something you find, it is something you are." The nature of the Self is happiness.

After knowing who you are, the next question in the evolution of consciousness is "why am I here?" The search for the meaning and purpose of life is an age old quest. From Time immemorial, seekers have devoted their entire life to the pursuance of the quest to answer this question. As I set out on my personal quest to answer this question, I discovered a two part answer: every person has a purpose and mission in life.

The purpose of life is the same for all human beings. It is the mission of life that has as many possibilities as there are people. If you study nature the purpose of the caterpillar is to become a butterfly. If the caterpillar does not transform itself into a butterfly, it can be said that it did not fulfill its purpose in life. The purpose of all human life is to reach the state of self realization. This state is called by many different names by the different spiritual traditions. Some of the names for this state of Self Realization are: Enlightenment, Nirvana, God consciousness and God Realization. To bring people to this state was the mission of all of the avatars, prophets, saints, and perfect masters who have come to the world from the many different religions. Just as the caterpillar goes through certain stages of internal transformation to become a butterfly, there is a transformational process that a human beings can go through to reach this glorious state of Self Realization.

Alchemy is the science of changing base metals into gold. Spiritual alchemy is the science of transforming human qualities into God's qualities.

Why am I here? The purpose of human life is to develop God's qualities, and reach the state of Self Realization through the process of spiritual alchemy.

786

The Path

WALKING ON THIS PATH SOMETIMES IS

HECTIC

UPHILL

TRIALS SHOULD BE EXPECTED

TURN BACK, TURN BACK THE HANDS OF TIME

MIND OVER MATTER

MEDITATE TO STILL THE MIND

ILLUSION CLOUDS PERCEPTION

QUESTION

ARE YOU IN THE RIGHT DIRECTION?

DEATH IS A BRIDGE THAT MUST BE CROSSED

STUDY THE SIGNS NOW SO YOU WON'T BE LOST

THE SPIRIT PLANE

VIBRATES FASTER

KUNDALINI SHOULD ONLY BE RAISED

BY A MASTER

LIFE IS A GAME SIMILAR TO CHESS

STEP AWAY FROM THE GAME

AND YOU CAN SEE IT BEST

TAI CHI, MANTRA, DUALITY, YIN YANG

EASTERN PHILOSOPHY, SUFI, I CHING

RETURN OF THE JEDI, OPENING OF THE

3RD EYE

DIE B-4 U DIE

AND BECOME IMMORTAL

THE EGYPTIAN MYSTERIES HAVE BEEN

REVEALED

THIS IS THE TURNING OF THE SEVENTH

WHEEL

HIDDEN WISDOM FOR THE MASSES IN

AQUARIUS

RISE UP SANKOFA

THE PHOENIX WILL FLY AGAIN

WE ARE EXPERIENCING TOTAL RECALL

OF HIGHER PLANES OF EXISTENCE

BEFORE THE FALL

THE MATRIX IS REAL

THIS IS A HOLOGRAPHIC UNIVERSE

THE THEORY OF RELATIVITY MUST BE

REVERSED

LIGHT UPON LIGHT

EXPERIENCE THE TRANSMISSION

WHAT WILL IT TAKE

TO RAISE OUR CONDITION

THE PATH

786

Light Upon Light

Ancient sufi mystics have said time and time again "the entire universe is light". Einstein's theory of relativity is a restatement of this ancient wisdom in a scientific formula. $E=mc^2$ means if matter (m) is multiplied by the speed of light squared(c^2) it will turn into energy

(E). Light is a form of energy. Thus the theory of relativity restated also means that if light, energy is slowed down, it will turn into matter. Thus the vibration of light slowed down creates matter. God is light. God is the creator and sustainer of the universe. IN the beginning was the word, God, Light. The word, God, became flesh, the universe/man. The vibration of the light and sound of God, slowed down, created and manifested the universe, and all that it contains, including man/woman. The science of spiritual alchemy is the reversal of this process, returning matter(man) to its original state of origin, energy(God).

My mother used to say

Every day for several years, when my brother and I would leave the house to go to school, or anywhere, we would hear these words from our mother "Make good decisions. Think positive." Without fail, as we grew up, these words became our mantra as we went out into the world. As a young child if I was going down the street to play with friends I would hear "Make good decisions. Think positive." As I got older and got my first job on my way to work I would hear "Make good decisions. Think positive." My mother repeated this mantra so much that when I went away to college, on my way to class, in the back of my mind I would hear her voice saying " Make good decisions. Think positive." Even today still I can hear her loving voice saying "Make good decisions.

Think positive." Looking back on my life I can see the power of making good decisions, and positive thinking.

For many many years I have pondered why did my mother use those exact words every day? My mother was a student of christian metaphysics, so I grew up on a heavy diet of Emmet Fox, Neville and Joel Goldsmith. After re-reading some of their works, and others, as an adult I found that what she was doing was firmly rooting in me and my brother the power of choice and positive thinking. A proverb says "The man who thinks he can and the man who thinks he can not, are both right."

It is the power of choice that gives man free will. It is free will, the power to choose between right and wrong that makes man higher than the angels. Free will, the power of choice, is one of the greatest gifts from God to man.

I often say "Life is a choice, make a good one". Life is full of choices. The choices you make today greatly influence your tomorrow. If you want a good tomorrow (future) make a good choice today (now). Example: If you know you have a test tomorrow, a good choice would be to study today, which will influence your test scores tomorrow.

The power of choice has several implications in life. Making good decisions today, and thinking positively about the outcome, has a dramatic affect on our future. The present is pre-sent by the past thoughts words and actions that we choose.

The eagle and the chicken

There once was an eagle who was born and raised in a chicken coop. The eagle did not know it was an eagle. It thought it was a chicken! In fact it had never seen an eagle before. As the eagle grew up with the chickens it paid no attention to the fact that it was a little taller than the chickens. But it did notice that it's wings were quite larger and different than the others. As the story goes, the eagle ate the same food as the chickens. It learned to scratch the ground and look for corn and worms. It even learned to speak the language of the chickens! One day another eagle was flying over the chicken coop. To it's surprise and amazement it looked down to see, an eagle looking for food with the chickens. It said to itself "Am I dreaming? Is that a full grown eagle in the chicken coop?" The eagle immediately turned around, flew back, and landed on top of the barnyard to observe the strange phenomenon. As he observed the situation he could not believe it. He called out from the top of the barn to the other eagle "Hey you, yea you, the tall one with the big wings."

"Are you talking to me?" said the other eagle.

"Yes, do you know you are an eagle who can fly high in the sky and leave the chicken coop any time you get ready?" Upon hearing this, the other eagle laughed so hard he fell over on the ground. "You mean I can fly? Please, please stop joking" said the other eagle. At this point the eagle on top of the barn flew down into the chicken coop, grabbed the other eagle and flew to the top of a nearby tree. "You can definitely fly just like me" he said. Spread your wings out.

"Wow" said the other eagle, as he spread his wings out. I always knew my wings were different, but I never spread them out because I did not want the other chickens to notice.

"Other chickens!" shouted the eagle. Raising his voice he said, "You are not a chicken you are an eagle. Take off and fly!
"

" I can't!"

"You can and you will fly" the eagle shouted and pushed him off the tree branch! As he was falling to the ground by natural instinct, he flapped his wings, started to fly and was never seen again!

786

Half empty or Half full

One day on the subway in Philadelphia, a friend and EYE were discussing the concept of the glass half empty or half full. I noticed a young man across from us paying attention to our conversation. When I said "There is no spoon" (a line from the Matrix) the guy across from us said "What spoon and what glass are you talking about?" This of course became a teaching moment.

Visualize a glass of water in front of you that is half full of water. Ask yourself the question "Is the glass half full or half empty?" The answer to the question will determine your outlook on life. Whether you know it or not, consciousness shapes reality. Your reality is the objectification of your state of consciousness. If you see the glass as half empty then you have a pessimistic, negative outlook on life. If you see the glass as half full you have an optimistic , positive outlook on life. If you see the glass as an illusion, and God as the only REALITY then you have the mind of a mystic. Your mind state and what you believe and view as real have a direct effect on your experience.

Research shows, from several projects, that placebo medicine can have a healing effect on people in a study if they believe it is real medicine.

"As a man thinketh in his heart, so is he." "As above, so below". "On earth as it is in heaven." As above, and as it is in heaven , refer to consciousness, belief, and the spiritual plane. So below, and on earth refer to the physical plane of existence.

Before anything can manifest on earth, the physical plane, it must first exist on the spiritual plane in the world of ideas and belief. " The Kingdom of heaven is within." Within refers to your consciousness. It is not a physical place. "On earth as it is in heaven" means that which is first conceived by the minds eye, can be manifested here on the earth. Therefore we have the metaphysical concept "Thoughts are forms." So I ask you is the glass half empty or half full? Just by believing and affirming in your state of consciousness that the glass is half full, you will begin to produce more abundance in your life. "My cup runneth over."

Divine Mind

Divine Mind Shine. Your thoughts words and actions create/determine your experience/ Reality. The pre-sent is pre SENT by your past thoughts words and actions. Your thoughts determine your experience. All is consciousness/mind. On earth as it is in heaven. The inner meaning of this prayer is earth=manifestation, heaven=mind. As above so below has the same esoteric meanings/implications. All things on the physical plane(below/earth) first manifest on the mental plane(above) from the spiritual plane(heaven). The great Avatar Jesus has said in the Bible "the kingdom of heaven is within you." The spirit plane(heaven) is pure consciousness. We shape the spiritual plane by our thoughts. All and everything exist in potential form on the spiritual plane. Our thoughts/consciousness give shape/form to the potential realities that exist on the spiritual plane.

Divine Mind Shine. Thoughts manifest in

Time. Divine Mind does not make a distinction between so-called good and evil (duality). In the state of the Divine Mind there is only ONENESS. You reap what you sow. To "sow" means to plant ideas thoughts on the plane of Divine Mind. In time you will "reap" see in your life the actual manifestations of what exists in your mind, thoughts. Thoughts of abundance produce abundance. Thoughts of poverty produce poverty. Focusing the mind is like tuning into a frequency on a radio station. When you tune into a jazz station you hear jazz music. When you tune into a rap station you hear garbage, excuse me rap music LOL. Back to the subject.....You would not expect to hear rock and roll when you tune into a nice jazz station. It is the same with our thought. We must first learn to tune into Divinity. Learn to cultivate what eye call the Divine Mind. When we cultivate this Divine Mind, all other things will be added. "Seek first the kingdom of heaven, and all things will be added." In the Holy Quran God says "I do not change a condition of a people until they first change that which is WITHIN themselves." Think, act and most of all BE positive!!!

Divine Mind Science

"On earth as it is in heaven." The kingdom of heaven is within you." "He calleth things that are not seen as though they were and things that were not seen become seen." – The Bible

"Man will surely have what he strives for." "All things will cease to exist except for the face of Allah." "I do not change a condition of a people until they first change that which is within themselves." – The Quran

"Thought is the forerunner of all actions." The Buddha

"The nature of God(Brahman) is OM(PRIMORDIAL SOUND) SAT(TRUTH) CHI(CONSCIOUSNESS) ANANDA(BLISS). YOU ARE THAT."- Hindu Advaita philosophy

Today we are going to enter into one of my favorite subjects: the Science of Mind. My mother was into Christian metaphysics, so eye was raised on a steady diet of Ernest Holmes, Joel Goldsmith, Mary Baker Eddy, and Neville. This science is most important for all people regardless of what their religion is because it deals with one of man's most important possessions: the mind. As a child eye was taught that the power of God was within ME. Eye was never taught to believe in a mystery God that was up in heaven somewhere, outside of my SELF.

"The world, and all within it, is mans consciousness objectified. Consciousness is the cause as well as the substance of the entire world. Consciousness in the ONE and only reality." – Neville, Resurrection page 46

The ONENESS of Consciousness manifest a dual nature on this plane of existence. The two divisions of Consciousness are the conscious mind, and the subconscious mind. The conscious mind is masculine. The subconscious mind is feminine. The subconscious mind is the womb of creation the gives birth to our reality based on the impressions it receives from the conscious mind. "I do not change the condition of a people until they first change that which is within themselves." That which must be changed inside a person to change their outer experience is the subconscious mind. Man transmits ideas to the subconscious mind through feelings and repetition. A feeling must be felt over and over again until it is impressed on the subconscious mind. When it is impressed on the subconscious mind, it will be manifest of the physical plane. In order to change our reality we must first learn to control our thoughts and feelings which create patterns on the subconscious mind. In a short lecture to a few close friends eye once explained the idea of the virgin birth/immaculate conception. Immaculate conception takes place when you have an idea or desire you want to manifest on the physical plane, and by assuming the feeling of what it would feel like when the idea/desire is manifest you create the seed that is planted into the womb of the subconscious mind. In time(which is an illusion) this seed-idea-thought form- will be born on the physical plane in the form of a virgin birth. Feeling a thing AS IF IT ALREADY EXIST is the KEY!!! Magic is the ability/power to take a thought form and make it manifest on the physical plane.

"Imagination is the beginning of the growth of all forms, and faith is the substance out of which they are formed. By imagination, that which exists in latency or is asleep within the deep of consciousness is awakened and given form." – Neville "Faith is the substance of things hoped for, the evidence of things not seen." The soul of man is masculine, and is related to the conscious mind. The spirit of man is feminine and is related to the sub consciousness. One tantric key for manifestation is for the soul(conscious mind) to make love with the spirit(subconscious mind), thus giving birth to a new reality. All things exist on the spirit plane before they manifest on the physical plane. We use the conscious mind to access the spirit through prayer and meditation. By faith it is done to you. Belief creates reality. When you develop the power within yourself to believe in things that are unseen, regardless of outer appearance, these things that you believe in will manifest. In the Quran God has said "This is the book for those who believe in the unseen." Our beloved prophet Muhammad(peace be upon him) has said "pray to Allah with faith that Allah will answer your prayer." In the Quran God has said "I answer the prayer of those who believe in Me." The sufi says "pray to Allah with the feeling that your prayer has already been answered." FEELING & BELIEF are the keys of manifestation.

Happiness IS

Deep

inside my heart

a still voice

sings

a soliloquy of

Bliss

captivated by the melody

eye exist

in a state

of

extreme

HAPPINESS!!!!

Eye once asked one of my teachers what it would take to find happiness? He looked at me, smiled and said "happiness is not something you find. Happiness

is something you ARE." Part of the true nature of the human being is

Bliss(ananda). This Blissful nature is an aspect of God, who is seen in the hindu

tradition as Sat(truth) Chi(consciousness) and Bliss(ananda). Since God is the

true Self, Bliss is an aspect of Self. Bliss also translates as happiness! True

happiness does NOT come from any outside source, like: money, relationships,

sex, or drugs. True happiness comes from the Self/God. True happiness is not

something that comes and goes based on outer circumstances. True happiness

is ETERNAL because God, its source is eternal!!! Eye once saw a church

billboard that said "if God seems far away, who moved?" In the Bible

the Holy Avatar Jesus said

that the kingdom of heaven is within, and we all know that God is in heaven so

God must BE within U. The prophet Muhammad said "God cannot fit into the

heavens or the earth, but God fits into the hearts of His believers." The search

for happiness is untimely the search for God!

Ironically looking for God is like a fish in the ocean looking for water LOL. Be

still and KNOW that God, happiness is an aspect of your true nature. All u have

to do

is find Self, and you will have found God and HAPPINESS…..

Live more , Laugh more, Love more!!!------ sufi ananda

www.786sufiwisdom.com

CHEIKH AHMADOU BAMBA

AND

CHEIKH IBRA FALL

SUFI MEDITATION TECHNIQUE

LEVEL 1 & 2

www.786sufiwisdom.com.

These techniques were developed by Qiyamah Abdallah Salihu-sufi ananda.

Diciple of Cheikh Ahmadou Bamba

Copyright 786 Sufi Wisdom 2012

786..."be still and Know that I am God."---The Bible
Level 1
To know the Self is to know God. When we learn to still the mind we can know God. God is a Light inside of your heart. In reality you are one with that Light..."Allah is the Light of the heavens and the earth."--The Quran. The heavens represents the mind, and the earth represents the body/the heart....

Sufi Meditation made easy: sit facing the east 2 times a day and say:(out loud or silent)

La ee la ha ill Allah for 10 minutes.
It means:
God is the only One worthy of worship. It also means God is the only reality.
At the end of the 10 minutes say:
Muhammad dur rasool lu la. 1 time
it means:
Muhammad is a prophet of God.

After one week of practice, extend the time period to 20min. At the end of the third week extend the time to 30minutes. If done twice a day, over time, this will begin to purify your heart and you mind.
It is good to burn some type of incense during the meditation. A sufi is meditation in motion. Try to find a way to take your meditation with you wherever you go, repeat the meditation in your mind at all times. The goal is to be in constant Union with God.

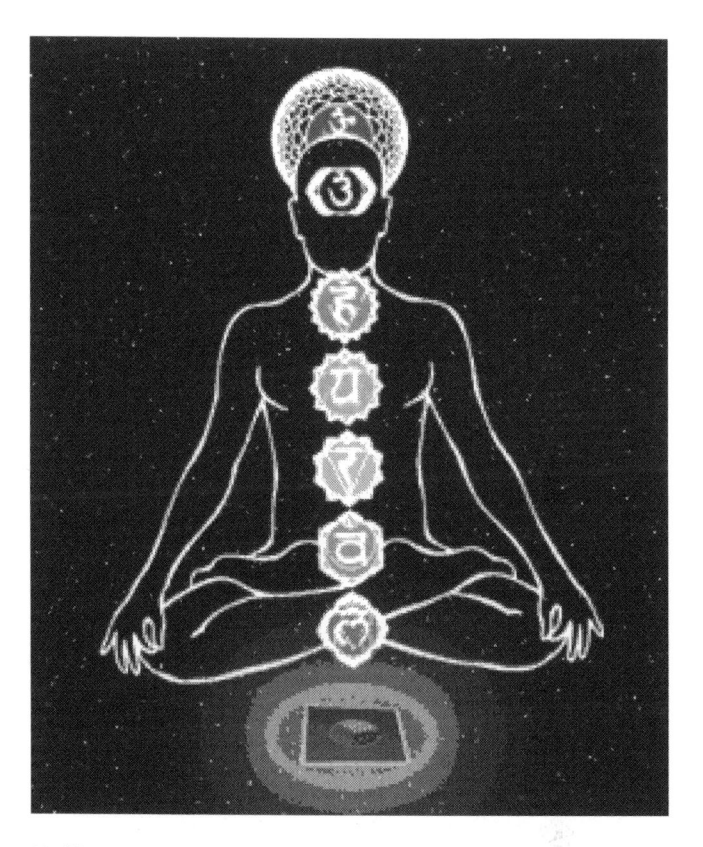

7 Chakra purification with La ee la ha ill Allah: Level 2 meditation with creative visualization.

There are 7 energy centers located from the base of the spine to the top of the head. These 7 centers a part of the ethereal body and are called chakras. LA ee la ha ill Ah la has 7 syllables. During this meditation, with eyes closed each of the 7 syllables of La ee la ha in Ah la is said In ascending order visualizing one of the 7 syllables In/on one of the 7 chakras. La ee la ha ill Ah La Is visualized entering into the body at the base of the spine with one of the 7 syllables being placed on each of the chakras as it travels though the ethereal body.

- LA – at the base of spine – 1st chakra
- EE- genital area – 2nd chakra
- LA- stomach area - 3rd chakra
- HA- inside the heart – 4th chakra
- ILL- in the throat – 5th chakra
- AH- in the 3rd eye(center of forehead) -6th chakra
- LA – top, center of head – 7th chakra

Let the visualization be easy. Try not to use too much mind force. The 7 syllables should be seen emitting a radiant white LIGHT that expands as it enters into each chakra. This LIGHT expands and contracts as it moves from the base of the spine (1st chakra) to the top of the head (7th chakra). If you have any questions about this technique feel free to call or email sufi at: sufimystic7@yahoo.com or 267-560-SUFI(7834)

Made in the USA
Coppell, TX
31 May 2021